Civilisation: Its Cause

by Edward Carp

The friendly and flowing savage, who is he? Is he waiting for civilisation, or is he past it, and mastering it? --Whitman

We find ourselves today in the midst of a somewhat peculiar state of society, which we call Civilisation, but which even to the most optimistic among us does not seem altogether desirable. Some of us, indeed, are inclined to think that it is a kind of disease which the various races of man have to pass through--as children pass through measles or whooping cough; but if it is a disease, there is this serious consideration to be made, that while History tells us of many nations that have been attacked by it, of many that have succumbed to it, and of some that are still in the throes of it, we know of no single case in which a nation has fairly recovered from and passed through it to a more normal and healthy condition. In other words the development of human society has never yet (that we know of) passed beyond a certain definite and apparently final stage in the process we call Civilisation; at that stage it has always succumbed or been arrested.

Of course it may at first sound extravagant to use the word disease in connection with Civilisation at all, but a little thought should show that the association is not ill-grounded. To take the matter on its physical side first, I find that in Mullhall's Dictionary of Statistics (1884) the number of accredited doctors and surgeons in the United Kingdom is put at over 23,000. If the extent of the national sickness is such tht we require 23,000 medical men to attend to us, it must surely be rather serious! And they do not cure us. Wherever we look today, in mansion or in slum, we see the features and hear the complaints of ill-health; the difficulty is really to find a healthy person. The state of the modern civilised man in this respect-our coughs, colds, mufflers, dread of a waft of chill air, etc.--is anything but creditable, and it seems to be the fact that, notwithstanding all our libraries of medical science, our knowledges, arts, and appliances of life, we are actually less capable of taking care of ourselves than the animals are. Indeed, talking of animals, we are-as Shelley I think points out-fast depraving the domestic breeds. The cow, the horse, the sheep, and even the confiding pussy-cat, are becoming ever more and more subject to disease, and are liable to ills which in their wilder state they knew not of. And finally the savage races of the earth do not escape the baneful influence. Wherever Civilisation touches them, they die like flies from the smallpox, drink, and worse evils it brings along with it, and often its mere contact is enough to destroy whole races.

But the word Disease is applicable to our social as well as to our physical condition. For as in the body disease arises from the loss of the physical unity which constitutes Health, and so takes the form of warfare or discord between the various parts, or of the abnormal development of individual organs, or the consumption of the system by predatory germs and growths; so in our modern life we find the unity gone which constitutes true society, and in its place warfare of classes and individuals, abnormal development of some to the detriment of others, and consumption of the organism by masses of social parasites. If the word disease is applicable anywhere, I should say it is-both in its direct and its derived sense-to the civilised societies of today.

Again, mentally, is not our condition most unsatisfactory? I am not alluding to the number and importance of the lunatic asylums which cover our land, nor to the fact that maladies of the brain and nervous system are now so common; but to the strange sense of mental unrest which marks our populations, and which amply justifies Ruskin's cutting epigram: that our two objects in life are, "Whatever we have-to get more; and wherever we are-to go somewhere else." This sense of unrest, of disease, penetrates down even into the deepest regions of man's being-into his moral nature-disclosing itself there, as it has done in all nations notably at the time of their full civilisation, as the sense of Sin.[1] All down the Christian centuries we find this strange sense of inward strife and discord developed, in marked contrast to the naive insouciance of the pagan and primitive world; and, what is strangest., we even find people glorying in this consciousness-which, while it may be the harbinger of better things to come, is and can be in itself only the evidence of loss of unity, and therefore of ill-health, in the very centre of human life.

Of course we are aware with regard to Civilisation that the word is sometimes used in a kind of ideal sense, as to indicate a state of future culture towards which we are tending-the implied assumption being that a sufficiently long course of top hats and telephones will in the end bring us to this ideal condition; while any little drawbacks in the process, such as we have just pointed out, are explained as being merely accidental and temporary. Men sometimes speak of civilising and ennobling influences as if the two terms were interchangeable, and of course they have a right to use the word Civilisation in this sense if they like; but whether the actual tendencies of modern life taken in the mass are ennobling (except in a quite indirect way hereafter to be dwelt upon) is, to say the least, a doubtful question. Anyone who would get an idea of the glorious being that is as a matter of fact being turned out by the present process should read Mr. Kay Robinson's article in the Nineteenth Century for May, 1883, in which he prophesies (quite solemnly and in the name of science) that the human being of the future will be a toothless, bald, toeless creature with flaccid muscles and limbs almost incapable of locomotion!

Perhaps it is safer on the whole not to use the word Civilisation in such ideal sense, but to limit its use (as is done today by all writers on primitive society) to a definite historical stage through which the various nations pass, and in which we actually find ourselves at the present time. Though there is of course a difficulty in marking the commencement of any period of historical evolution very definitely, yet all students of this subject agree that the growth of property and the ideas and institutions flowing from it did at a certain point bring about such a change in the structure of human society that the new stage might fairly be distinguished from the earlier stages of Savagery and Barbarism by a separate term. The growth of Wealth, it is shown, and with it the concept of Private Property, brought on certain very definite new forms of social life; it destroyed the ancient system of society based upon the gens, that is, a society of equals founded upon blood-relationship, and introduced a society of classes founded upon differences of material possession; it destroyed the ancient system of mother-right and inheritance through the female line, and turned the woman into the property of the man; it brought with it private ownership of land, and so created a class of landless aliens, and a whole system of rent, mortgage, interest, etc.; it introduced slavery, serfdom and wage-labour, which are only various forms of the dominance of one class over another; and to rivet these authorities it created the State and the policeman.

Every race that we know that has become what we call civilised, has passed through these changes; and though the details may vary and have varied a little, the main order of change has been practically the same in all cases. We are justified therefore in calling Civilisation a historical stage, whose commencement dates roughly from the division of society into classes founded on property and the adoption of class-government. Lewis Morgan in his Ancient Society adds the invention of writing and the consequent adoption of written History and written Law; Engels in his Ursprung der Familie, des Privateigenthums und des Staats points out the importance of the appearance of the Merchant, even in his most primitive form, as a mark of the civilisationperiod; while the French writers of the last century made a good point in inventing the term nations polliceés (policemanised nations) as a substitute for civilised nations; for perhaps there is no better or more universal mark of the period we are considering, and of its social degradation, than the appearance of the crawling phenomenon in question. [Imagine the rage of any decent North American Indians if they had been told they required policemen to keep them in order!]

If we take this historical definition of Civilisation, we shall see that our English Civilisation began hardly more than a thousand years ago, and even so the remains of the more primitve society lasted long after that. In the case of Rome-if we reckon from the later times of the early kings down to the fall of Rome-we have again about a thousand years. The Jewish civilisation from David and Solomon downwards lasted-with breaks-somewhat over a thousand years; the Greek civilisation less; the series of Egyptian civilisations which we can now distinguish lasted altogether very much longer; but the important points to see are, first, that the process has been quite similar in character in these various (and numerous other) cases,[2] quite as similar in fact as the course of the same disease in various persons; and secondly that in no case, as said before, has any nation come through and passed beyond this stage; but that in most cases it has succumbed soon after the main symptoms had been developed.

But it will be said, It may be true that Civilisation regarded as a stage of human history presents some features of disease; but is there any reason for supposing that disease in some form or other was any less present in the previous stage-that of Barbarism? To which I reply, I think there is good reason. Without committing ourselves to the unlikely theory that the "noble savage" was an ideal human being physically or in any other respect, and while certain that in many points he was decidely inferior to the civilised man, I think we must allow him the superiority in some directions; and one of these was his comparative freedom from disease. Lewis Morgan, who grew up among the Iroquois Indians, and who probably knew the North American natives as well as any white man has ever done, says (in his Ancient Society, p. 45), "Barbarism ends with the production of grand Barbarians." And though there are no native races on the earth today who are actually in the latest and most advanced stage of Barbarism;[3] yet, if we take the most advanced tribes that we know of-such as the said Iroquois Indians of twenty or thirty years ago, some of the Kaffir tribes round Lake Nyassa in Africa, now (and possibly for a few years more) comparatively untouched by civilisation, or the tribes along the river Uaupes, thirty or forty years back, of Wallace's Travels on the Amazon-all tribes in what Morgan would call the middle stage of Barbarism-we undoubtedly in each case discover a fine and (which is our point here) heathy people. Captain Cook in his first Voyage says of the natives of Otaheite, "We saw no critical disease during our stay upon the island, and but few instances of sickness, which were accidental fits of the colic;" and, later on, of the New Zealanders, "They enjoy perfect and uninterrupted health. In all our visits to their towns, where young and old, men and women, crowded about us... we never saw a single person who appeared to have any bodily complaint, nor among the numbers we have seen naked did we once perceive the slightest eruption upon the skin, or any marks that an eruption had left behind." These are pretty strong words. Of course diseases exist among such peoples, even where they have never been in contact with civilisation, but I think we may say that among the higher types of savages they are rarer, and nothing like so various and so prevalent as they are in our modern life; while the power of recovery from wounds (which are of course the most frequent form of disablement) is generally admitted to be something astonishing. Speaking of the Kaffirs, J. G. Wood says, "Their state of health enables them to survive injuries which would be almost instantly fatal to any civilised European." Mr. Frank Qates in his Diary[4] mentions the case of a man who was condemned to death by the king. He was hacked down with axes, and left for dead. "What must have been intended for the coup de grâce was a cut in the back of the head, which had chipped a large piece out of the skull, and must have been meant to cut the spinal cord where it joins the brain. It had, however, been made a little higher than this, but had left such a wound as I should have thought that no one could have survived... when I held the lanthorn to investigate the wound I started back in amazement to see a hole at the base of the skull, perhaps two inches long and an inch and a half wide, and I will not venture to say how deep, but the depth too must have been an affair of inches. Of course this hole penetrated into the substance of the brain, and probably for some distance. I dare say a mouse could have sat in it." Yet the man was not so much disconcerted. Like Old King Cole, "He asked for a pipe and a drink of brandy," and ultimately made a perfect recovery! Of course it might be said that such a story only proves the lowness of organization of the brains of savages; but to the Kaffirs at any rate this would not apply; they are a quick-witted race, with large brains, and exceedingly acute in argument, as Colenso found to his cost. Another point which indicates superabundant health is the amazing animal spirits of these native races! The shouting, singing, dancing kept up nights long among the Kaffirs are exhausting merely to witness, while the graver North American Indian exhibits a corresponding power of life in his eagerness for battle or his stoic resistance of pain.[5]

Similarly when we come to consider the social life of the wilder races-however rudimentary and undeveloped it may be-the almost universal testimony of students and travellers is that within its limits it is more harmonious and compact than that of the civilised nations. The members of the tribe are not organically at warfare with each other; society is not divided into classes which prey upon each other; nor is it consumed by parasites. There is more true social unity, less of disease. Though the customs of each tribe are rigid, absurd, and often frightfully cruel,[6] and though all outsiders are liable to be regarded as enemies, yet within those limits the members live peacefully together-their pursuits, their work, are undertaken in common, thieving and violence are rare, social feeling and community of interest are strong. "In their own bands, Indians are perfectly honest. In all my intercourse with them I have heard of not over half-a-dozen cases of such theft. But this wonderfully exceptional honesty extends no further than to the members of his immediate band. To all outside of it, the Indian is not only one of the most arrant thieves in the world, but this quality or faculty is held in the highest estimation." (Dodge, p. 64.) If a man set out on a journey (this among the Kaffirs) "he need not trouble himself about provisions, for he is sure to fall in with some hut, or perhaps a village, and is equally sure of obtaining both food and shelter."[7] "I have lived," says A. R. Wallace in his Malay Archipelago (vol. ii, p. 460), "with communities in South America and the East, who have no laws or law courts, but the public opinion of the village... yet each man scrupulously respects the rights of his fellows, and any infraction of those rights rarely takes place. In such a community all are nearly equal. There are none of those wide distinctions of education and ignorance, wealth and poverty, master and servant, which are the product of our civilisation." Indeed this community of life in the early societies, this absence of division into classes, and of the contrast between rich and poor, is now admitted on all sides as a marked feature of difference between the conditions of the primitive and of civilised man.[8]

Lastly, with regard to the mental condition of the Barbarian, probably no one will be found to dispute the contention that he is more easy-minded and that his consciousness of Sin is less developed than in his civilised brother. Our unrest is the penalty we pay for our wider life. The missionary retires routed from the savage in whom he can awake no sense of his supreme wickedness. An American lady had a servant, a negro-woman, who on one occasion asked leave of absence for the next morning, saying she wished to attend the Holy Communion. "I have no objection," said the mistress, "to grant you leave; but do you think you ought to attend Communion? You know you have never said you were sorry about that goose you stole last week." "Lor' missus," replied the woman, "do ye think I'd let an old goose stand betwixt me and my Blessed Lord and Master?" But joking apart, and however necessary for man's ultimate evolution may be the temporary development of this consciousness of Sin, we cannot help seeing that the condition of the mind in which it is absent is the most distinctively healthy; nor can it be concealed that some of the greatest works of Art have been produced by people like the earlier Greeks, in whom it was absent; and could not possibly have been produced where it was strongly developed.

Though, as already said, the latest stage of Barbarism, i.e., that just preceding Civilisation, is unrepresented on the earth today, yet we have in the Homeric and other dawn-literature of the various nations indirect records of this stage; and these records assure us of a condition of man very similar to, though somewhat more developed than, the condition of the existing races I have mentioned above. Besides this, we have in the numerous traditions of the Golden Age,[9] legends of the Fall, etc., a curious fact which suggests to us that a great number of races in advancing towards Clyilisation were conscious at some point or other of having lost a primitive condition of ease and contentment, and that they embodied this consciousness, with poetical adornment and licence, in imaginative legends of the earlier Paradise. Some people indeed, seeing the universality of these stories, and the remarkable fragments of wisdom embedded in them and other extremely ancient myths and writings, have supposed that there really was a general pre-historic Eden-garden or Atlantis: but the necessities of the case hardly seem to compel this supposition. That each human soul, however, bears within itself some kind of reminiscence of a more harmonious and perfect state of big which it has at some time experienced, seems to me a conclusion difficult to avoid; and this by itself might give rise to manifold traditions and myths.

II

However all this may be, the question immediately before us-having established the more healthy, though more limited, condition of the precivilisation peoples-is, Why this lapse or fall? What is the meaning of this manifold and intensified manifestation of Disease-physical, social, intellectual, and moral? What is its place and part in the great whole of human evolution?

And this involves us in a digression, which must occupy a few pages, on the nature of Health.

When we come to analyse the conception of Disease, physical or mental, in society or in the individual, it evidently means, as already hinted once or twice, loss of unity. Health, therefore, should mean unity, and it is curious that the history of the word entirely corroborates this idea. As is well known, the words health, whole, holy, are from the same stock; and they indicate to us the fact that far back in the past-those who created this group of words had a conception of the meaning of Health very different from ours, and which they embodied unconsciously in the word itself and its strange relatives.

These are, for instance, and among others: heal, hallow, hale, holy, whole, wholesome; German heilig, Heiland (the Saviour); Latin salus (as in salutation, salvation); Greek kalos; also compare hail! a salutation, and, less certainly connected, the root hal, to breathe, as in inhale, exhale-French haleine-Italian and French alma and âme (the soul); compare the Latin spiritus, spirit or breath, and Sanskrit atman, breath or soul.

Wholeness, holiness... "if thine eye be single, thy whole body shall be full of light."... "thy faith hath made thee whole."

The idea seems to be a positive one-the condition of the body in which it is an entirety, a unity-a central force maintaining that condition; and disease being the break-up-or break-down-of that entirety into multiplicity.

The peculiarity about our modern conception of Health is that it seems to be a purely negative one. So impressed are we by the myriad presence of Disease-so numerous its dangers, so sudden and unforetellable its attacks-that we have come to look upon health as the mere absence of the same. As a solitary spy picks his way through a hostile camp at night, sees the enemy sitting round his fires, and trembles at the crackling of a twig beneath his feet-so the traveller through this world, comforter in one hand and physic-bottle in the other, must pick his way, fearful lest at any time he disturb the sleeping legions of death-thrice blessed if by any means, steering now to the right and now to the left, and thinking only of his personal safety, he passed by without discovery to the other side.

Health with us is a negative thing. It is a neutralisation of opposing dangers. It is to be neither rheumatic nor gouty, consumptive nor bilious, to be untroubled by headache, backache, heartache, or any of the "thousand natural shocks that flesh is heir to." These are the realities. Health is the mere negation of them.

The modern notion, and which has evidently in a very subtle way penetrated the whole thought of today, is that the essential fact of life is the existence of innumerable external forces, which, by a very delicate balance and difficult to maintain, concur to produce Man-who in consequence may at any moment be destroyed again by the non-concurrence of those forces. The older notion apparently is that the essential fact of life is Man himself: and that the external forces, so-called, are in some way subsidiary to this fact-that they may aid his expression or manifestation, or that they may hinder it, but that they can neither create nor annihilate the Man. Probably both ways of looking at the subject are important; there is a man that can be destroyed, and there is a man that cannot be destroyed. The old words, soul and body, indicate this contrast; but like all words they are subject to the defect that they are an attempt to draw a line where no line can ultimately be drawn; they mark a contrast where, in fact, there is only continuity-for between the little mortal man who dwells here and now, and the divine and universal Man who also forms a part of our consciousness, is there not a perfect gradation of being, and where (if anywhere) is there a gulf fixed? Together they form a unit, and each is necessary to the other: the first cannot do without the second, and the second cannot get along at all without the first. To use the words of Angelus Silesius (quoted by Schopenhauer), "Ich weiss dass ohne mich Gott nicht ein Nu kann leben."

According then to the elder conception, and perhaps according to an elder experience, man, to be really healthy, must be a unit, an entirety-his more external and momentary self standing in some kind of filial relation to his more universal and incorruptible part-so that not only the remotest and outermost regions of the body, and all the assimilative, secretive, and other processes belonging thereto, but even the thoughts and passions of the mind itself, stand in direct and clear relationship to it, the final and absolute transparency of the mortal creature. And thus this divinity in each creature, being that which constitutes it and causes it to cohere together, was conceived of as that creature's saviour, healer-healer of wounds of body and wounds of heart-the Man within the man, whom it was not only possible to know, but whom to know and be united with was the alone salvation. This, I take it, was the law of health-and of holiness-as accepted at some elder time of human history, and by us seen as thro' a glass darkly.

And the condition of disease, and of sin, under the same view, was the reverse of this. Enfeeblement, obscuration, duplicity-the central radiation blocked; lesser and insubordinate centres establishing and asserting themselves as against it; division, discord, possession by devils.

Thus in the body, the establishment of an insubordinate centre-a boil, a tumor, the introduction and spread of a germ with innumerable progeny throughout the system, the enlargement out of all reason of an existing organ-means disease. In the mind, disease begins when any passion asserts itself as an independent centre of thought and action. The condition of health in the mind is loyalty to the divine Man within it.[10] But if loyalty to money become an independent centre of life, or greed of knowledge, or of fame, or of drink; jealousy, lust, the love of approbation; or mere following after any so-called virtue for itself-purity, humility, consistency, or what not-these may grow to seriously endanger the other. They are, or should be, subordinates; and though over a long period their insubordination may be a necessary condition of human progress, yet during all such time they are at war with each other and with the central Will; the man is torn and tormented, and is not happy.

And when I speak thus separately of the mind and body, it must be remembered, as already said, that there is no strict line between them; but probably every affection or passion of the mind has its correlative in the condition of the body-though this latter may or may not be easily observable. Gluttony is a fever of the digestive apparatus. What is a taint in the mind Is also a taint in the body. The stomach has started the original idea of becoming itself the centre of the human system. The sexual organs may start a similar idea. Here are two distinct threats, menaces made against the central authority-against the Man himself. For the man must rule or disappear; it is impossible to imagine a man presided over by a Stomach-a walking Stomach, using hands, feet, and all other members merely to carry it from place to place, and serve its assimilative mania. We call such a one an Hog. [And thus in the theory of Evolution we see the place of the hog, and all other animals, as forerunners or off-shoots of special faculties in Man, and why the true man, and rightly, has authority over all animals, and can alone give them their place in creation.]

So of the Brain, or any other organ; for the Man is no organ, resides in no organ, but is the central life ruling and radiating among all organs, and assigning them their parts to play.

Disease then, in body or mind, is from this point of view the break-up of its unity, its entirety, into multiplicity. It is the abeyance of a central power, and the growth of insubdrdinate centres-life in each creature being conceived of as a continual exercise of energy or conquest, by which external or antagonistic forces (and organisms) are brought into subjection and compelled into the service of the creature, or are thrown off as harmful to it. Thus, by way of illustration, we find that plants or animals, when in good health, have a remarkable power of throwing off the attacks of any parasites which incline to infest them; while those that are weakly are very soon eaten up by the same. A rose-tree, for instance, brought indoors, will soon fall a prey to the aphis-though when hardened out of doors the pest makes next to no impression on it. In dry seasons when the young turnip plants in the fields are weakly from want of water the entire crop is sometimes destroyed by the turnip fly, which multiplies enormously; but if a shower or two of rain come before much damage is done the plant will then grown vigorously, its tissues become more robust and resist the attacks of the fly, which in its turn dies. Late investigation seems to show that one of the functions of the white corpuscles in the blood is to devour disease germs and bacteria present in the circulation-thus absorbing these organisms into subjection to the central life of the body-and that, with this object they congregate in numbers toward any part of the body which is wounded or diseased. Or to take an example from society, it is clear enough that if our social life were really vivid and healthy, such parasitic products as the idle shareholder and the policeman above-mentioned would simply be impossible. The material on which they prey would not exist, and they would either perish or be transmuted into useful forms. It seems obvious in fact that life in any organism can only be maintained by some such processes as these-by which parasitic or infesting organisms are either thrown off or absorbed into subjection. To define the nature of the power which thus works towards and creates the distinctive unity of each organism may be difficult, is probably at present impossible, but that some such pomer exists we can hardly refuse to admit. Probably it is more a subject of the growth of our consciousness, than an object of external scientific investigation.

In this view, Death is simply the loosening and termination of the action of this power-over certain regions of the organism; a process by which, when these superficial parts become hardened and osseous, as in old age, or irreparably damaged, as in cases of accident, the inward being sloughs them off, and passes into other spheres. In the case of man there may be noble and there may be ignoble death, as there may be noble and ignoble life. The inward self, unable to maintain authority over forces committed to its charge, declining from its high prerogative, swarmed over by parasites, and fallen partially into the clutch of obscene foes, may at last with shame and torment be driven forth from the temple in which it ought to have been supreme. Or, having fulfilled a holy and wholesome time, having radiated divine life and love through all the channels of body and mind, and as a perfect workman uses his tools, so having with perfect mastery and nonchalance used all the materials committed to it, it may quietly and peacefully lay these down, and unchanged (absolutely unchanged to all but material eyes) pass on to other spheres appointed.

And now a few words on the medical aspect of the subject. If we accept any theory (even remotely similar to that just indicated) to the effect that Health is a positive thing, and not a mere negation of disease, it becomes pretty clear that no mere investigation of the latter will enable us to find out what the former is, or bring us nearer to it. You might as well try to create the ebb and flow of the tides by an organised system of mops.

Turn your back upon the Sun and go forth into the wilderness of space till you come to those limits where the rays of light, faint with distance, fall dimly upon the confines of eternal darkness-and phantoms and shadows in the half-light are the product of the wavering conflict betwixt day and night-investigate these shadows, describe them, classify them, record the changes which take place in them, erect in vast libraries these records into a monument of human industry and research; so shall you be at the end as near to a knowledge and understanding of the sun itself-which all this time you have left behind you, and on which you have turned your back-as the investigators of disease are to a knowledge and understanding of what health is. The solar rays illumine the outer world and give to it its unity and entirety; so in the inner world of each individual possibly is there another Sun, which illumines and gives unity to the man, and whose warmth and light would permeate his system. Wait upon the shining forth of this inward sun, give free access and welcome to its rays of love, and free passage for them into the common world around you, and it may be you will get to know more about health than all the books of medicine contain, or can tell you.

Or to take the former simile: it is the central force of the Moon which acting on the great ocean makes all its waters one, and causes them to rise and fall in timely consent. But take your moon away; hey! now the tide is flowing too far down this estuary! Station your thousands with mops, but it breaks through in channel and runlet! Block it here, but it overflows in a neighboring bay! Appoint an army of swabs there, but to what end? The infinitest care along the fringe of this great sea can never do, with all imaginable dirt and confusion, what the central power does easily, and with unerring grace and providence.

And so of the great (the vast and wonderful) ocean which ebbs and flows within a man—take away the central guide—and not 20,000 doctors, each with 20,000 books to consult and 20,000 phials of different contents to administer, could meet the myriad cases of disease which would ensue, or bolster up into "wholeness" the being from whom the single radiant unity had departed.

Probably there has never been an age, nor any country (except Yankee-land?) in which disease has been so generally prevalent as in England today; and certainly there has never (with the same exception) been an age or country in which doctors have so swarmed, or in which medical science has been so powerful, in apparatus, in learning, in authority, and in actual organisation and number of adherents. How reconcile this contradiction—if indeed a contradiction it be?

But the fact is that medical science does not contradict disease—any more than laws abolish crime. Medical science—and doubtless for very good reasons—makes a fetish of disease, and dances around it. It is (as a rule) only seen where disease is; it writes enormous tomes on disease; it induces disease in animals (and even men) for the purpose of studying it; it knows to a marvelous extent the symptoms of disease, its nature, its causes, its goings out and its comings in; its eyes are perpetually fixed on disease, till disease (for it) becomes the main fact of the world and the main object of its worship. Even what is so gracefully called Hygiene does not get beyond this negative attitude. And the world still waits for its Healer, who shall tell us-diseased and suffering as we are-what health is, where it is to be found, whence it flows; and who having touched this wonderful power within himself shall not rest till he has proclaimed and imparted it to men.

No, medical science does not, in the main, contradict disease. The same cause (infidelity and decay of the central life in men) which creates disease and makes men liable to it, creates students and a science of the subject. The Moon[11] having gone from over the waters, the good people rush forth with their mops; and the untimely inundations, and the mops and the mess and the pother, are all due to the same cause.

As to the lodgement of disease, it is clear that this would take place easily in a disorganised system-just as a seditious adventurer would easily effect a landing, and would find insubordinate materials ready at hand for his use, in a land where the central government was weak. And as to the treatment of a disease so introduced, there are obviously two methods: one is to reinforce the central power till it is sufficiently strong of itself to eject the insubordinate elements and restore order; the other is to attack the malady from outside and if possible destroy it-(as by doses and decoct ions)- independently of the inner vitality, and leaving that as it was before. The first method would seem the best, most durable and effective; but it is difficult and slow. It consists in the adoption of a healthy life, bodily and mental, and will be spoken of later on. The second may be characterised as the medical method, and is valuable, or rather I should be inclined to say, will be valuable, when it has found its place, which is to be subsidiary to the first. It is too often, however, regarded as superior in importance, and in this way, though easy of application, has come perhaps to be productive of more harm than good. The disease may be broken down for the time being, but the roots of it not being destroyed, it soon springs up again in the same or a new form, and the patient is as badly off as ever.

The great positive force of Health, and the power which it has to expel disease from its neighborhood is a thing realised, I believe, by few persons. But it has been realised on earth, and will be realised again when the more squalid elements of our present-day civilisation have passed away.

III

The result then of our digression is to show that Health-in body or mind-means unity, integration as opposed to disintegration. In the animals we find this physical unity existing to a remarkable degree. An almost unerring instinct and selective power rules their actions and organisation. Thus a cat before it has fallen (say before it has become a very wheezy fireside pussy!) is in a sense perfect. The wonderful consent of its limbs as it runs or leaps, the adaptation of its muscles, the exactness and inevitableness of its instincts, physical and affectional; its senses of sight and smell, its cleanliness, nicety as to food, motherly tact, the expression of its whole body when enraged, or when watching for prey-all these things are so to speak absolute and instantaneous-and fill one with admiration. The creature is "whole" or in one piece: there is no mentionable conflict or division within it.[12]

Similarly with the other animals, and even with the early man himself. And so it would appear returning to our subject-that, if we accept the doctrine of evolution, there is a progression of animated beings-which, though not perfect, possess in the main the attribute of health-from the lowest forms up to a healthy and instinctive though certainly limited man. During all this stage the central law is in the ascendant, and the physical frame of each creature is the fairly clean vehicle of its expression-varying of course in complexity and degree according to the point of unfoldment which has been reached. And when thus in the long process of development the inner Man (which has lain hidden or dormant within the animal) at last appears, and the creature consequently takes on the outer frame and faculties of the human being, which are only as they are because of the inner man which they represent; when it has passed through stage after stage of animal life, throwing out tentative types and likenesses of what is to come, and going through innumerable preliminary exercises in special forms and faculties, till at last it begins to be able to wear the full majesty of manhood itself-then it would seem that that long process of development is drawing to a close, and that the goal of creation must be within measurable distance.

But then, at that very moment, and when the goal is, so to speak, In sight, occurs this failure of "wholeness" of which we have spoken, this partial break-up of the unity of human nature-and man, instead of going forward any longer in the same line as before, to all appearance falls.

What is the meaning of this loss of unity? What is the cause and purpose of this fall and centuries-long exile from the earlier Paradise? There can be but one answer. It is self-knowledge-(which involves in a sense the abandonment of self). Man has to become conscious of his destiny-to lay hold of and realise his own freedom and blessedness-to transfer his consciousness from the outer and mortal part of him to the inner and undying.

The cat cannot do this. Though perfect in its degree, its interior unfoldment Is yet incomplete. The human soul within it has not yet come forward and declared itself; some sheathing leaves have yet to open before the divine flower-bud can be clearly seen. And when at last (speaking as a fool) the cat becomes a man-when the human soul within the creature has climbed itself forward and found expression, transforming the outer frame in the process into that of humanity-(which is the meaning I suppose of the evolution theory)-then the creature, though perfect and radiant in the form of Man, still lacks one thing. It lacks the knowledge of itself; it lacks its own identity, and the realisation of the manhood to which as a fact it has attained.

In the animals consciousness has never returned upon itself. It radiates easily outwards; and the creature obeys without let or hesitation, and with little or any self-consciousness, the law of its being. And when man first appears on the earth, and even up to the threshold of what we call civilisation, there is much to show that he should in this respect still be classed with the animals. Though vastly superior to them in attainments, physical and mental, in power over nature, capacity of progress, and adaptability, he still in these earlier stages was like an animal in the unconscious instinctive nature of his action; and on the other hand, though his moral and intellectual structures were far less complete than those of the modern man-as was a necessary result of the absence of self-knowledge-he actually lived more in harmony with himself and with nature,[13] than does his descendant; his impulses, both physical and social, were clearer and more unhesitating; and his unconsciousness of inner discord and sin a great contrast to our modern condition of everlasting strife and perplexity.

If then to this stage belongs some degree of human perfection and felicity, yet there remains a much vaster height to be scaled. The human soul which has wandered darkling for so many thousands of years, from its tiny spark-like germ In some low form of life to its full splendor and dignity in man, has yet to come to the knowledge of its wonderful heritage, has yet to become fully individualised and free, to know itself immortal, to resume and interpret all its past lives, and to enter in triumph into the kingdom which it has won.

It has in fact to face the frightful struggle of self-consciousness, or the disentanglement of the true self from the fleeting and perishable self. The animals and man, unfallen, are healthy and free from care, but unaware of what they are; to attain self-knowledge man must fall; he must become less than his true self; he must endure imperfection; division and strife must enter his nature. To realise the perfect Life, to know what, how wonderful it is-to understand that all blessedness and freedom consists in its possession-he must for the moment suffer divorce from it; the unity, the repose of his nature must be broken up; crime, disease and unrest must enter in, and by contrast he must attain to knowledge.

Curious that at the very dawn of the Greek and with it the European civilisation we have the mystic words "Know Thyself" inscribed on the temple of the Delphic Apollo; and that first among the legends of the Semitic race stands that of Adam and Eve eating of the tree of Knowledge of good and evil! To the animal there is no such knowledge, and to the perfected man of the future there will be no such knowledge. It is a temporary perversion, indicating the disunion of the present-day man-the disunion of the outer self from the inner-the horrible dual self-consciousness-which is the means ultimately of a more perfect and conscious union than could ever have been realised without it-the death that is swallowed up in victory. "For the first man is of the earth, earthy; but the second man is the Lord from heaven."

In order then, at this point in his evolution, to advance any farther, man must first fall; in order to know, he must lose. In order to realise what Health is, how splendid and glorious a possession, he must go through all the long negative experience of Disease; in order to know the perfect social life, to understand what power and happiness to mankind are involved in their true relation to each other, he must learn the misery and suffering which come from mere individualism and greed; and in order to find his true Manhood, to discover what a wonderful power it is, he must first lose it-he must become a prey and a slave to his own passions and desires-whirled away like Phaeton by the horses which he cannot control.

This moment of divorce, then, this parenthesis in human progress, covers the ground of all history; and the whole of Civilisation, and all crime and disease, are only the materials of its immense purpose-themselves destined to pass away as they arose, but to leave their fruits eternal.

Accordingly we find that it has been the work of Civilisation-founded as we have seen on property-in every way to disintegrate and corrupt man-literally to corrupt-to break up the unity of his nature. It begins with the abandonment of the primitive life and the growth of the sense of shame (as in the myth of Adam and Eve). From this follows the disownment of the sacredness of sex. Sexual acts cease to be a part of religious worship; love and desire-the inner and the outer love-hitherto undifferentiated, now become two separate things. (This no doubt a necessary stage in order for the development of the consciousness of love, but in itself only painful and abnormal.) It culminates and comes to an end, as today, in a complete divorce between the spiritual reality and the bodily fulfilment-in a vast system of commercial love, bought and sold, in the brothel and in the palace. It begins with the forsaking of the hardy nature-life, and it ends with a society broken down and prostrate, hardly recognisable as human, amid every form of luxury, poverty and disease. He who had been the free child of Nature denies his sonship; he disowns the very breasts that suckled him. He deliberately turns his back upon the light of the sun, and hides himself away in boxes with breathing holes (which he calls houses), living ever more and more in darkness and asphyxia, and only coming forth forth perhaps once a day to blink at the bright god, or to run back again at the first breath of the free wind for fear of catching cold! He muffles himself in the cast-off furs of the beasts, every century swathing himself in more and more layers, more and more fearfully and wonderfully fashioned, till he ceases to be recognisable as the Man that was once the crown of the animals, and presents a more ludicrous spectacle than the monkey that sits on his own barrel organ. He ceases to a great extent to use his muscles, his feet become partially degenerate, his teeth wholly, his digestion so enervated that he has to cook his food and make pulps of all his victuals, and his whole system so obviously on the decline that at last in the end of time a Kay Robinson arises and prophesies as aforesaid, that he will before long become totally toothless, bald and toeless.

And so with this denial of nature comes every form of disease; first delicatesse, daintiness, luxury; then unbalance, enervation, huge susceptibility to pain. With the shutting of himself away from the all-healing Power, man inevitably weakens his whole manhood; the central bond is loosened, and he falls a prey to his own organs. He who before was unaware of the existence of these latter, now becomes only too conscious of them (and this-is it not the very object of the process?); the stomach, the liver and the spleen start out into painful distinctness before him, the heart loses its equable beat, the lungs their continuity with the universal air, and the brain becomes hot and fevered; each organ in turn asserts itself abnormally and becomes a seat of disorder, every corner and cranny of the body becomes the scene and symbol of disease, and Man gazes aghast at his own kingdom- whose extent he had never suspected before-now all ablaze in wild revolt against him. And then-all going with this period of his development-sweep vast epidemic trains over the face of the earth, plagues and fevers and lunacies and world-wide festering sores, followed by armies, ever-growing, of doctors-they too with their retinues of books and bottles, vaccinations and vivisections, and grinning death's-heads in the rear-a mad crew, knowing not what they do, yet all unconsciously, [no doubt], fulfilling the great age-long destiny of humanity.

In all this the influence of Property is apparent enough. It is evident that the growth of property through the increase of man's powers of production reacts on the man in three ways: to draw him away namely (1) from Nature, (2) from his true Self, (3) from his Fellows. In the first place it draws him away from Nature. That is, that as man's power over materials increases he creates for himself a sphere and an environment of his own, in some sense apart and different from the great elemental world of the winds and the waves, the woods and the mountains, in which he has hitherto lived. He creates what we call the artificial life, of houses and cities, and, shutting himself up in these, shuts Nature out. As a growing boy at a certain point, and partly in order to assert his independence, wrests himself away from the tender care of his mother, and even displays-just for the time being-a spirit of opposition to her, so the growing Man finding out his own powers uses them-for the time-even to do despite to nature, and to create himself a world In which she shall have no part. In the second place the growth of propert draws man away from his true Self. This is clear enough. As his power over materials and his possessions increases, man finds the means of gratifying his senses at will. Instead of being guided any longer by that continent and "whole" instinct which characterises the animals, his chief motive is now to use his powers to gratify this or that sense or desire. These become abnormally magnified, and the man soon places his main good in their satisfaction; and abandons his true Self for his organs, the whole for the parts. Property draws the man outwards, stimulating the external part of his being, and for a time mastering him, overpowers the central Will, and brings about his disintegration and corruption. Lastly, property by thus stimulating the external and selfish nature in man, draws him away from his Fellows. In the anxiety to possess things for himself, in order to gratify his own bumps, he is necessarily brought into conflict with his neighbor and comes to regard him as an enemy. For the true Self of man consists in his organic relation with the whole body of his fellows; and when the man abandons his true Self he abandons also his true relation to his fellows. The mass-Man must rule in each unit-man, else the unit-man will drop off and die, but when the outer man tries to separate himself from the inner, the unit-man from the mass-Man, then the reign of individuality begins-a false and impossible individuality of course, but the only means of coming to the consciousness of the true individuality. With the advent of a Civilisation then founded on Property the unity of the old tribal society is broken up. The ties of blood relationship which were the foundation of the gentile system and the guarantees of the old fraternity and equality become dissolved in favor of powers and authorities founded on mere possession. The growth of Wealth disintegrates the ancient Society; the temptations of power, of possession, etc., which accompany it, wrench the individual from his moorings; personal greed rules; "each man for himself" becomes the universal motto; the hand of every man is raised against his brother, and at last society itself becomes an organisation by which the rich fatten upon the vitals of the poor, the strong upon the murder of the weak. [It is interesting in this connection to find that Lewis Morgan makes the invention of a written alphabet and the growth of the conception of private property the main characteristics of the civilisation-period as distinguished from the periods of savagery and barbarism which preceded it; for the invention of writing marks perhaps better than anything else could do the period when Man becomes self-conscious-when he records his own doings and thoughts, and so commences History proper; and the growth of private property marks the period when he begins to sunder himself from his fellows, when therefore the conception of sin (or separation) first enters in, and with it all the long period of moral perplexity, and the denial of that community of life between himself and his fellows which is really the essence of man's being.]

And then arises the institution of Government.

Hitherto this had not existed except in a quite rudimentary form. The early communities troubled themselves little about individual ownership, and what government they had was for the most part essentially democratic-as being merely a choice of leaders among blood-relations and social equals. But when the delusion that man can exist for himself alone-his outer and, as it were, accidental self apart from the great inner and cosmical self by which he is one with his fellows-when this delusion takes possession of him, it is not long before it finds expression in some system of private property. The old community of life and enjoyment passes away, and each man tries to grab the utmost he can, and to retire into his own lair for its consumption. Private accumulations arise; the natural flow of the bounties of life is dammed back, and artificial barriers of Law have to be constructed in order to preserve the unequal levels. Outrage and Fraud follow in the wake of the desire of possession; force has to be used by the possessors in order to maintain the law-barriers against the non-possessors; classes are formed; and finally the formal Government arises, mainly as the expression of such force; and peserves itself, as best it can, until such time as the inequalities which it upholds become too glaring, and the pent social waters gathering head burst through once more and regain their natural levels.

Thus Morgan in his Ancient Society points out over and over again that the civilised state rests upon territorial and property marks and qualifications, and not upon a personal basis as did the ancient gens, or the tribe; and that the civilised government correspondingly takes on quite a different character and function from the simple organisation of the gens. He says (p. 124), "Monarchy is incompatible with gentilism." Also with regard to the relation of Property to Civilisation and Government he makes the following pregnant remarks (p. 505): "It is impossible to over-estimate the influence of property in the civilisation of mankind. It was the power that brought the Aryan and Semitic nations out of barbarism into civilisation. The growth of the idea of property in the human mind commenced in feebleness and ended in becoming its master passion. Governments and Laws are instituted with primary reference to its creation, protection and enjoyment. It introduced human slavery as an instrument in its production; and after the experience of several thousand years it caused the abolition of slavery upon the discovery that a freeman was a better property-making machine." And in another passage on the same subject, "The dissolution of society bids fair to become the termination of a career of which property is the end and aim; because such a career contains the elements of self-destruction. Democracy is the next higher plane. It will be a revival in a higher form of the liberty, equality, and fraternity of the ancient gentes."

The institution of Government is in fact the evidence in social life that man has lost his inner and central control, and therefore must resort to an outward one. Losing touch with the inward Man-who is his true guide-he declines upon an external law, which must always be false. If each man remained in organic adhesion to the general body of his fellows, no serious disharmony could occur; but it is when this vital unity of the body politic becomes weak that it has to be preserved by artificial means, and thus it is that with the decay of the primitive and instinctive social life there springs up a form of government which is no longer the democratic expression of the life of the whole people; but a kind of outside authority and compulsion thrust upon them by a ruling class or caste.

Perhaps the sincerest, and often though not always the earliest, form of Government is Monarchy. The sentiment of human unity having been already partly but not quite lost, the people choose-in order to hold society together- a man to rule over them who has this sentiment in a high degree. He represents the true Man and therefore the people. This is often a time of extensive warfare and the formation of nations. And it is interesting in this connection to note that the quite early "Kings" or leaders of each nation just prior to the civilisation period were generally associated with the highest religious functions, as in the case of the Roman rex, the Greek basileus, the early Egyptian Kings, Moses among the Israelites, and Druid leaders of the Britons, and so on.

Later, and as the central authority gets more and more shadowy in each man, and the external attraction of Property greater, so it does in society. The temporal and spiritual powers part company. The king-who at first represented the Divine Spirit or soul of society, recedes into the background, and his nobles of high degree (who may be compared to the nobler, more generous, qualities of the mind) begin to take his place. This is the Aristocracy and the Feudal Age-the Timocracy of Plato; and is marked by the appearance of large private tenures of land, and the growth of slavery and serfdom-the slavery thus outwardly appearing in society being the symbol of the inward enslavement of the man.

Then comes the Commercial Age-the Oligarchy or Plutocracy of Plato. Honour quite gives place to material wealth; the rulers rule not by personal or hereditary, but by property qualifications. Parliaments and constitutions and general Palaver are the order of the day. Wage-slavery, usury, mortgages, and other abominations, indicate the advance of the mortal process. In the individual man gain is the end of existence; industry and scientific cunning are his topmost virtues.

Last of all the break-up is complete. The individaul loses all memory and tradition of his heavenly guide and counterpart; his nobler passions fail for want of a leader to whom to dedicate themselves; his industry and his intellect serve but to minister to his little swarming desires. This is the era of anarchy-the democracy of Carlyle; the rule of the rabble, and mob-law; caucuses and cackle, competition and universal greed, breaking out in cancerous tyrannies and plutocracies-a mere chaos and confusion of society. For just as we saw in the human body, when the inner and positive force of Health has departed from it, that it falls a prey to parasites which overspread and devour it; so, when the central inspiration departs out of social life, does it writhe with the mere maggots of individual greed, and at length fall under the dominion of the most monstrous egotist who has been bred from its corruption.

Thus we have briefly sketched the progress of the symptoms of the "disease," which, as said before, runs much (though not quite) the same course in the various nations which it attacks. And if this last stage were really the end of all, and the true Democracy, there were indeed little left to hope for. No words of Carlyle could blast that black enough. But this is no true Democracy. Here in the "each for himself" is no rule of the Demos in every man, nor anything resembling it. Here is no solidarity such as existed in the ancient tribes and primaeval society, but only disintegration and a dust-heap. The true Democracy has yet to come. Here in this present stage is only the final denial of all outward and class government, in preparation for the restoration of the inner and true authority. Here in this stage the task of civilisation comes to an end; the purport and object of all these centuries is fulfilled; the bitter experience that mankind had to pass through is complete; and out of this Death and all the torture and unrest which accompanies it, comes at last the Resurrection. Man has sounded the depths of alienation from his own divine spirit, he has drunk the dregs of the cup of suffering, he has literally descended into Hell; henceforth he turns, both in the individual and in society, and mounts deliberately and consciously back again towards the unity which he has lost.[14]

And the false democracy parts aside for the disclosure of the true Democracy which has been formed beneath it-which is not an external government at all, but an inward rule-the rule of the mass-Man in each unit-man. For no outward government can be anything but a make-shift-a temporary hard chrysalis-sheath to hold the grub together while the new life is forming inside-a device of the civilisation-period. Farther than this it cannot go, since no true life can rely upon an external support, and, when the true life of society comes, all its forms will be fluid and spontaneous and voluntary.

IV

And now, by way of a glimpse into the future-after this long digression what is the route that man will take?

This is a subject that I hardly dare tackle. "The morning wind ever blows," says Thoreau, "the poem of creation is uninterrupted-but few are the ears that hear it." And how can we, gulfed as we are in this present whirlpool, conceive rightly the glory which awaits us? No limit that our present knowledge puts need alarm us; the impossibilities will yield very easily when the time comes; and the anatomical difficulty as to how and where the wings are to grow will vanish when they are felt sprouting!

It can hardly be doubted that the tendency will be-indeed is already showing itself-towards a return to nature and community of human life. This is the way back to the lost Eden, or rather forward to the new Eden, of which the old was only a figure. Man has to undo the wrappings and the mummydom of centuries, by which he has shut himself from the light of the sun and lain in seeming death, preparing silently his glorious resurrection-for all the world like the funny old chrysalis that he is. He has to emerge from houses and all his other hiding places wherein so long ashamed (as at the voice of God in the garden) he concealed himself-and Nature must once more become his home, as it is the home of the animals and the angels.

As it is written in the old magical formula: "Man clothes himself to descend, unclothes himself to ascend." Over his spiritual or wind-like body he puts on a material or earthy body; over his earth-body he puts on the skins of animals and other garments; then he hides this body in a house behind curtains and stone walls-which become to it as secondary skins and prolongations of itself. So that between the man and his true life there grows a dense and impenetrable hedge; and, what with the cares and anxieties connected with his earth-body and all its skins, he soon loses the knowledge that he is a Man at all; his true self slumbers in a deep and agelong swoon.

But the instinct of all who desire to deliver the divine imago within them is, in something more than the literal sense, towards unclothing. And the process of evolution or exfoliation itself is nothing but a continual unclothing of Nature, by which the perfect human Form which is at the root of it comes nearer and nearer to its manifestation.

Thus, in order to restore the Health which he has lost, man has in the future to tend in this direction. Life indoors and in houses has to become a fraction only, instead of the principal part of existence as it is now. Garments similarly have to be simplified. How far this process may go it is not necessary now to enquire. It is sufficiently obvious that our domestic life and clothing may be at once greatly reduced in complexity, and with the greatest advantage-made subsidiary instead of being erected into the fetishes which they are. And everyone may feel assured that each gain in this direction is a gain in true life-whether it be the head that goes uncovered to the air of heaven, or the feet that press bare the magnetic earth, or the elementary raiment that allows through its meshes the light itself to reach the vital organs. The life of the open air, familiarity with the winds and waves, clean and pure food, the companionship of the animals-the very wrestilng with the great Mother for his food-all these things will tend to restore that relationship which man has so long disowned; and the consequent instreaming of energy into his system will carry him to perfections of health and radiance of being at present unsuspected.

Of course, it will be said that many of these things are difficult to realise in our country, that an indoor life, with all its concomitants, is forced upon us by the climate. But if this is to some small-though very small-extent true, it forms no reason why we should not still take advantage of every opportunity to push in the direction indicated. It must be remembered, too, that our climate is greatly of our own creation. If the atmosphere of many of our great towns and of the lands for miles in their neighborhood is devitalised and deadly-so that in cold weather it grants to the poor mortal no compensating power of resistance, but compels him at peril of his life to swathe himself in greatcoats and mufflers-the blame is none but ours. It is we who have covered the lands with a pall of smoke, and are walking to our own funerals under it.

That this climate, however, at its best may not be suited to the highest developments of human life is quite possible. Because Britain has been the scene of some of the greatest episodes of civilisation, it does not follow that she will keep the lead in the period that is to follow; and the Higher Communities of the future will perhaps take their rise in warmer lands, where life is richer and fuller, more spontaneous and more generous, than it can be here.

Another point in this connection is the food question. For the restoration of the central vigor when lost or degenerate, a diet consisting mainly of fruits and grains is most adapted. Animal food often gives for the time being a lot of nervous energy-and may be useful for special purposes; but the energy is of a spasmodic feverish kind; the food has a tendency to inflame the subsidiary centres, and so to diminish the central control. Those who live mainy on animal food are specially liable to disease-and not only physically; for their minds also fall more easily a prey to desires and sorrows. In times therefore of grief or mental trouble of any kind, as well as in times of bodily sickness, immediate recourse should be had to the more elementary diet. The body under this diet endures work with less fatigue, is less susceptible to pain, and to cold; and heals its wounds with extraordinary celerity; all of which facts point in the same direction. It may be noted, too, that foods of the seed kind-by which I mean all manner of fruits, nuts, tubers, grains, eggs, etc. (and I may include milk in its various forms of butter, cheese, curds, and so forth), not only contain by their nature the elements of life in their most condensed forms, but have the additional advantage that they can be appropriated without injury to any living creature-for even the cabbage may inaudibly scream when torn up by the roots and boiled, but the strawberry plant asks us to take of its fruit, and paints it red expressly that we may see and devour it! Both of which considerations must convince us that this kind of food is most fitted to develop the kernel of man's life.

Which all means cleanness. The unity of our nature being restored, the instinct of bodily cleanness, both within and without, which is such a marked characteristic of the animals, will again characterise mankind-only now instead of a blind instinct it will be a conscious, joyous one; dirt being only disorder and obstruction. And thus the whole human being, mind and body, becoming clean and radiant from its inmost center to its farthest circumference-"transfigured"-the distinction between the words spiritual and material disappears. In the words of Whitman, "objects gross and the unseen soul are one."

But this return to Nature, and identification in some sort with the great cosmos, does not involve a denial or depreciation of human life and interests. It is not uncommonly supposed that there is some kind of antagonism between man and nature, and that to recommend a life closer to the latter means mere asceticism and eremitism; and unfortunately this antagonism does exist today, though it certainly will not exist forever. Today it is unfortunately perfectly true that man is the only animal who, instead of adorning and beautifying, makes Nature hideous by his presence. The fox and the squirrel may make their homes in the wood and add to its beauty in so doing; but when Alderman Smith plants his villa there, the gods pack up their trunks and depart; they can bear it no longer. The Bushmen can hide themselves and become indistinguishable on a slope of bare rock; they twine their naked little yellow bodies together; and look like a heap of dead sticks; but when the chimney-pot hat and frock-coat appear, the birds fly screaming from the trees. This was the great glory of the Greeks that they accepted and perfected nature; as the Parthenon sprang out of the limestone terraces of the Acropolis, carrying the natural lines of the rock by gradations scarce perceptible into the finished and human beauty of frieze and pediment, and as, above, it was open for the, blue air of heaven to descend into it for a habitation; so throughout in all their best work and life did they stand in this close relation to the earth and the sky and to all instinctive and elemental the harmony of the landscape or the songs of the birds. Then the great temples, beautiful on every height, or by the shores of the rivers and the lakes, will be the storehouses of all precious and lovely things. There men, women and children will come to share in the great and wonderful common life, the gardens around will be sacred to the unharmed and welcome animals; there all store and all facilities of books and music and art for everyone, there a meeting place for social life and intercourse, there dances and games and feasts. Every village, every little settlement, will have such hall or halls. No need for. private accumulations. Gladly will each man, and more gladly still each woman, take his or her treasures, except what are immediately or necessarily in use, to the common center, where their value will be increased a hundred and a thousand fold by the greater number of those who can enjoy them, and where far more perfectly and with far less toil they can be tended than if scattered abroad in private hands. At one stroke half the labor and all the anxiety of domestic caretaking will be annihilated. The private dwelling places, no longer costly and labyrinthine in proportion to the value and number of the treasures they contain, will need no longer to have doors and windows jealously closed against fellow men or mother nature. The sun and air will have access to them, the indwellers will have unfettered egress. Neither man nor woman will be tied in slavery to the lodge which they inhabit; and in becoming once more a part of nature, the human habitation will at length cease to be what it is now for at least half the human race-a prison.

Men often ask about the new architecture-what, and of what sort, it is going to be. But to such a question there can be no answer till a new understanding of life has entered into people's minds, and then the answer will be clear enough. For as the Greek Temples and the Gothic Cathedrals were built by people who themselves lived but frugally as we should think, and were ready to dedicate their best work and chief treasure to the gods and common life; and as today when we must needs have for ourselves spacious and luxurious villas, we seem to be unable to design a decent church or public building; so it will not be until we once more find our main interest and life in the life of the community and the gods that a new spirit will inspire our architecture. Then when our temples and common halls are not designed to glorify an individual architect or patron, but are built for the use of free men and women, to front the sky and the sea and the sun, to spring out of the earth, companionable with the trees and the rocks, not alien in spirit from the sunlit globe Itself or the depth of the starry night-then I say their form and structure will quickly determine themselves, and men will have no difficulty in making them beautiful. And similarly with the homes or dwelling places of the people. Various as these may be for the various wants of men, whether for a single individual or for a family, or for groups of individuals or families, whether to the last degree simple, or whether more or less ornate and complex, still the new conception, the new needs of life, will necessarily dominate them and give them form by a law unfolding from within.

In such new human life then-its fields, its farms, its workshops, its cities-always the work of man perfecting and beautifying the lands, aiding the efforts of the sun and soil, giving voice to the desire of the mute earth-in such new communal life near to nature, so far from any asceticism or inhospitality, we are fain to see far more humanity and sociability than ever before: an infinite helpfulness and sympathy, as between the children of a common mother. Mutual help and combination will then have become spontaneous and instinctive: each man contributing to the service of his neighbor as inevitably and naturally as the right hand goes to help the left in the human body-and for precisely the same reason. Every man-think of it!-will do the work which he likes, which he desires to do, which is obviously before him to do, and which he knows will be useful, without thought of wages or reward; and the reward will come to him as inevitably and naturally as in the human body the blood flows to the member which is exerting itself. All the endless burden of the adjustments of labor and wages, of the war of duty and distaste, of want and weariness, will be thrown aside-all the huge waste of work done against the grain will be avoided; out of the endless variety of human nature will spring a perfectly natural and infinite variety of occupations, all mutually contributive; society at last will be free and the human being after long ages will have attained to deliverance.

This is the Communism which civilisation has always hated, as it hated Christ. Yet it is inevitable; for the cosmical man, the instinctive and elemental man accepting and crowning nature, necessarily fulfills the universal law of nature. As to External Government and Law, they will disappear; for they are only the travesties and transitory substitutes of Inward Government and Order. Society in its final state is neither a monarchy, nor an aristocracy nor a democracy, nor an anarchy, and yet in another sense it is all of these. It is an anarchy because there is no outward rule, but only an inward and invisible spirit of life; it is a democracy because it is the rule of the Mass-man, or Demos, in each unit man; it is an Aristocracy because there are degrees and ranks of such inward power in all men; and it is a Monarchy because all these ranks and powers merge in a perfect unity and central control at last. And so it appears that the outer forms of government which belong to the Civilisation-period are only the expression in separate external symbols of the facts of the true inner life of society.

And just as thus the various external forms of government during the Civilisation-period find their justification and interpretation in the ensuing period, so will it be with the mechanical and other products of the present time; they will be taken up, and find their proper place and use in the time to come. They will not be refused; but they will have to be brought into subjection. Our locomotives, machinery, telegraphic and postal systems; our houses, furniture, clothes, books, our fearful and wonderful cookery, strong drinks, teas, tobaccos; our medical and surgical appliances; high-faluting sciences and philosophies, and all other engines hitherto of human bewilderment, have simply to be reduced to abject subjection to the real man. All these appliances, and a thousand others such as we hardly dream of, will come in to perfect his power and increase his freedom; but they will not be the objects of a mere fetish-worship as now. Man will use them, instead of their using him. His real life will lie in a region far beyond them. But in thus for a moment denying and "mastering" the products of Civilisation, he will for the first time discover their true value, and reap from them an enjoyment unknown before.

The same with the moral powers. As said before, the knowledge of good and evil at a certain point passes away, or becomes absorbed into a higher knowledge. The perception of Sin goes with a certain weakness in the man. As long as there is conflict and division within him, so long does he seem to perceive conflict and opposing principles in the world without. As long as the objects of the outer world excite emotions in him which pass beyond his control, so long do those objects stand as the signals of evil-of disorder and sin. Not that the objects are bad in themselves, or even the emotions which they excite, but that all through this period these things serve to the man as indications of his weakness. But when the central power is restored in man and all things ate reduced to his service, it is impossible for him to see badness in anything. The bodily is no longer antagonistic to the spiritual love, but is absorbed into it. All his passions take their places perfectly naturally, and become, when the occasions arise, the vehicles of his expression. Vices under existing conditions are vices simply because of the inordinate and disturbing influence they exercise, but will cease again to be vices when the man regains his proper command. Thus Socrates having a clean soul in a clean body could drink his boon companions under the table and then go out himself to take the morning air-what was a blemish and defect in them being simply an added power of enjoyment to himself!

The point of difference throughout (being the transference of the center of gravity of life and consciousness from the partial to the universal man) is symbolised by the gradual resumption of more universal conditions. That is to say that during the civilisation-period, the body being systematically wrapped in clothes, the head alone represents man-the little finnikin, intellectual, self-conscious man in contra-distinction to the cosmical man represented by the entirety of the bodily organs. The body has to be delivered from its swathings in order that the cosmical consciousness may once more reside in the human breast. We have to become "all face" again-as the savage said of himself.[15]

Where the cosmic self is, there is no more self-consciousness. The body and what is ordinarily called the self are felt to be only parts of the true self, chief object of regard, but consclousaess is continually radiant from it, filling the body and overflowing upon external Nature. Thus the Sun in the physical world is the allegory of the true self. The worshiper must adore the Sun, he must saturate himself with sunlight, and take the physical Sun into himself. Those who live by fire and candlelight are filled with phantoms; their thoughts are Will-o'-th'-wisp-like images of themselves, and they are tormented by a horrible self-consciousness.

And when the Civilisation-period has passed away, the old nature-religion-perhaps greatly grown-will come back. This immense stream of religious life which, beginning far beyond the horizon of earliest history, has been deflected into various metaphysical and other channels-of Judaism, Christianity, Buddhism, and the like-during the historical period, will once more gather itself together to float on its bosom all the arks and sacred vessels of human progress. Man will once more feel his unity with his fellows, he will feel his unity with the animals, with the mountains and the streams, with the earth itself and the slow lapse of the constellations, not as an abstract dogma of Science or Theology, but as a living and ever-present fact. Ages back this has been better understood than now. Our Christian ceremonial is saturated with sexual and astronomical symbols; and long before Christianity existed, the sexual and astronomical were the main forms of religion. That is to say, men instinctively felt and worshiped the great life coming to them through Sex, the great life coming to them from the deeps of Heaven. They deified both. They placed their gods-their own human forms-in sex, they placed them in the sky. And not only so, but wherever they felt this kindred human life-in the animals, in the ibis, the bull, the lamb, the snake, the crocodile; in the trees and flowers, the oak, the ash, the laurel, the hyacinth; in the streams and waterfalls, on the mountain-sides or in the depths of the sea-they placed them. The whole universe was full of a life which, though not always friendly, was human and kindred to their own, felt by them, not reasoned about, but simply perceived. To the early man the nation of his having a separate individuality could only with difficulty occur; hence he troubled himself not with the suicidal questionings concerning the whence and whither which now vex the modern mind.[16] For what causes these questions to be asked is simply the wretched feeling of isolation, actual or prospective, which man necessarily has when he contemplates himself as a separate atom in this immense universe-the gulf which lies below seemingly ready to swallow him, and the anxiety to find some mode of escape. But when he feels once more that he, that he himself, is absolutely indivisibly and indestructibly a part of this great whole-why then there is no gulf into which he can possibly fall; when he is sensible of the fact, why then the how of its realisation, though losing none of its interest, becomes a matter for whose solution he can wait and work in faith and contentment of mind. The Sun or Sol, visible image of his very Soul, closest and most vital to him of all mortal things, occupying the illimitable heaven, feeding all with its life; the Moon, emblem and nurse of his own reflective thought, the conscious Man, measurer of Time, mirror of the Sun; the planetary passions wandering to and fro, yet within bounds; the starry destinies; the changes of the earth, and the seasons; the upward growth and unfoldment of all organic life; the emergence of the perfect Man, towards whose birth all creation groans and travails-all these things will return to become realities, and to be the frame or setting of his supra-mundane life. The meaning of the old religions will come back to him. On the high-tops once more gathering he will celebrate with naked dances the glory of the human form and the great processions of the stars, or greet the bright horn of the young moon which now after a hundred centuries comes back laden with such wondrous associations-all the yearnings and the dreams and the wonderment of the generations of mankind-the worship of Astarte and of Diana, of Isis or the Virgin Mary; once more in sacred groves will he reunite the passion and the delight of human love with his deepest feelings of the sanctity and beauty of Nature; or in the open, standing uncovered to the Sun, will adore the emblem of the everlasting splendor which shines within. The same sense of vital perfection and exaltation which can be traced in the early and pre-civilisation peoples-only a thousand times intensified, defined, illustrated and purified-will return to irradiate the redeemed and delivered Man.

In suggesting thus the part which Civilisation has played in history, I am aware that the word itself is difficult to define-is at best only one of those phantom-generalisations which the mind is forced to employ; also that the account I have given of it is sadly imperfect, leaning perhaps too much to the merely negative and destructive aspect of this thousand-year long lapse of human evolution. I would also remind the reader that though it is perfectly true that under the dissolving influence of civilisation empire after empire has gone under and disappeared, and the current of human progress time after time has only been restored again by a fresh influx of savagery, yet its corruptive tendency has never had a quite unlimited fling; but that all down the ages of its dominance over the earth we can trace the tradition of a healing and redeeming power at work in the human breast and an anticipation of the second advent of the son of man. Certain institutions, too, such as Art and the Family (though it seems not unlikely that both of these will greatly change when the special conditions of their present existence have disappeared), have served to keep the sacred flame alive; the latter preserving in island-miniatures, as it were, the ancient communal humanity when the seas of individualism and greed covered the general face of the earth; the former keeping up, so to speak, a navel-cord of contact with Nature, and a means of utterance of primal emotions else unsatisfiable in the world around.

And if it seem extravagant to suppose that Society will ever emerge from the chaotic condition of strife and perplexity in which we find it all down the lapse of historical time, or to hope that the civilisation-process which has terminated fatally so invariably in the past will ever eventuate in the establishment of a higher and more perfect health-condition, we may for our consolation remember that today there are features in the problem which have never been present before. In the first place, today civilisation is no longer isolated, as in the ancient world, in surrounding floods of savagery and barbarism, but it practically covers the globe, and the outlying savagery is so feeble as not possibly to be a menace to it. This may at first appear a drawback, for (it will be said) if Civilisation be not renovated by the influx of external savagery its own inherent flaws will destroy society all the sooner. And there would be some truth in this if it were not for the following consideration, namely, that while for the first time in History Civilisation is now practically continuous over the globe, now also for the first time can we descry forming in continuous line within its very structure the forces which are destined to destroy it and to bring about the new order. While hitherto isolated communisms, as suggested, have existed here and there and from time to time, now for the first time in History both the masses and the thinkers of all the advanced nations of the world are consciously feeling their way towards the establishment of a socialistic and communal life on a vast scale. The present competitive society is more and more rapidly becoming a mere dead formula and husk within which the outlines of the new and human society are already discernible. Simultaneously, and as if to match this growth, a move towards Nature and Savagery is for the first time taking place from within, instead of being forced on society from without. The nature movement begun years ago in literature and art is now, among the more advanced sections of the civilised world, rapidly realising itself in actual life, going so far even as a denial, among some, of machinery and the complex products of Civilisation, and developing among others into a gospel of salvation by sandals and sunbaths! It is in these two movements-towards a complex human communism and towards individual freedom and savagery-in some sort balancing and correcting each other, and both visibly growing up within, though utterly foreign to-our present-day Civilisation, that we have fair grounds, I think, for looking forward to its cure.

Footnotes

* It is interesting to note that the "sense of Sin" seems now (1920) to have nearly passed away. And this probably indicates a considerable impending change in our Social Order.

* For proof I must refer the reader to Engels, or to his own study of history.

* Say like the Homeric Greeks, or the Spartans of the Lycurgus period.

* Matabele Land and the Victoria Falls, p. 209.

* A similar physical health and power of life are also developed among Europeans who have lived for long periods in more native conditions. It is not to our race, which is probably superior to any in capacity, but to the state in which we live that we must ascribe our defect in this particular matter.

* See Col. Dodge's Our Wild Indians

* Wood's Natural History of Man

* See Appendix.

* See Note at end of this chapter.

* No words or theory even of morality can express or formulate this-no enthronement of any virtue can take its place; for all virtue enthroned before our humanity becomes vice, and worse than vice.

* It is curious that this word seems to have the same root as the word Man, the original idea apparently being Order, or Measure.

* And with regard to disease, though it is not maintained that among the animals there is anything like immunity from it-since diseases of a more or less parasitic character are common in all tribes of plants and animals-still they seem to be rarer, and the organic instinct of health greater, than in the civilised man.

* As to the unity of these wild races with nature, that is a matter seemingly beyond dispute; their keenness of sense, sensitiveness to atmospheric changes, knowledge of properties of plants and animals, etc., have been the subject of frequent remark; but beyond this, their strong feeling of union with the universal spirit, probably only dimly self conscious, but expressing itself very markedly and clearly in their customs, is most strange and pregnant of meaning. The dances of the Andaman Islanders on the sands at night, the wild festival of the new moon among the Fans and other African tribes, the processions through the forests, the chants and dull thudding of drums, the torture-dances of the young Red Indian bravos in the burning heat of the sun; the Dionysiac festivals among the early Greeks; and indeed the sacrificial nature-rites and carnivals and extraordinary powers of second-sight found among all primitive peoples; all these things indicate clearly a faculty which, though it had hardly become self-conscious enough to be what we call religion, was yet in truth the foundation element of religion, and the germ of some human powers which wait yet to be developed

* There is another point worth noting as characteristic of the civilisation period. This is the abnormal development of the abstract intellect compared with the physical senses on the one hand, and the moral sense on the other. Such a result might be expected, seeing that abstraction from reality is

naturally the great engine of that false individuality or apartness, which it is the object of Civilisation to produce. As it is, during this period man builds himself an intellectual world apart from the great actual universe around him; the "ghosts of things" are studied in books; the student lives indoors, he cannot face the open air-his theories "may prove very well in lecture rooms, yet not prove at all under the spacious clouds, and along the landscape and flowing currents"; children are "educated" afar from actual life; huge phantom-temples of philosophy and science are reared upon the most slender foundations; and In these he lives defended from actual facrt. For as a drop of water, when it comes in contact with red-hot iron, wraps itself in a cloud of vapor and is saved from destruction, so the little mind of man, lest it should touch the burning truth of Nature and God and be consumed, evolves at each point of contact a veil of insubstantial thought which allows it for a time to exist apart, and becomes the nurse of its self-consciousness

* See Alonso di Ovalle's Account of the Kingdom of Chile in Churchill's Collection of Voyages and Travels, 1724.

* See Notes at end of this chapter

Endnotes

(See p. 11) The following remarks by Mr H. B. Cotterill on the natives around Lake Nyassa, among whom he lived at a time, 1876-8, when the region was almost unvisited, may be of interest. "In regard of merely 'animal' development and well-being, that is in the delicate perfection of bodily faculties (perceptive), the African savage is as a rule incomparably superior to us. One feels like a child, utterly dependent on them, when travelling or hunting with them. It is true that many may be found (especially amongst the weaker tribes that have been slave-hunted or driven into barren corners) who are half-starved and wizened, but as a rule they are splendid animals. In character there is a great want of that strength which in the educated civilised man is secured by the roots striking out into the Past and Future-and in spite of their immense perceptive superiority they feel and acknowledge the superior force of character in the white man. They are the very converse of the Stoic self-sufficient sage-like children in their 'admiration' and worship of the Unknown. Hence their absolute want of Conceit, though they possess self-command and dignity. They are, to those they love and respect, faithful and devoted--their faithfulness and truthfulness are dictated by no 'categorical imperative,' but by personal affection. Towards an enemy they can be, without any conscientious scruples, treacherous and inhumanly cruel. I should say that there is scarcely any possible idea that is so foreign to the savage African mind as that of general philanthropy or enemy-love."

"In endurance the African savage beats us hollow (except trained athletes). On one occasion my men rowed my boat with 10 foot oars against the wind in a choppy sea for 25 hours at one go, across Kuwirwe Bay, about 60 miles. They never once stopped or left their seats--just handed round a handful of rice now and then. I was at the helm all the time--and had enough of it!... They carry 80 lbs. on their heads for 10 hours through swamps and jungles. Four of my men carried a sick man weighing 14 stones in a hammock for 200 miles, right across the dreaded Malikata Swamp. But for sudden emergencies, squalls, etc., they are nowhere."

(See p. 13) "So lovely a scene made easily credible the suggestion, otherwise highly probable, that the Golden Age was no mere fancy of the poets, but a reminiscence of the facts of social life in its primitive organisation of village and house-communities." (J. S. Stuart-Glenni's Europe and Asia, ch. i. Servia.)

(See p. 56) "It was only on the up-break of the primitive socialisms that the passionate desire of, and therefore belief in, individual Immortality arose. With an intense feeling, not of an independent individual life, but of a dependent common life, there is no passionate desire of, though there may be more or less of belief in, a continuance after death of individual existence." (Ibid., p. 161.)

Following is an extract from a letter from my friend Havelock Ellis, which he kindly allows me to reprint. The passage is interesting as indicating one cause, at any rate, of the failure of the modern civilisations. "Your remark that you are re-publishing Civilisation: Its Cause and Cure has led me to read it once again, and I see how well adapted it is for reissue just now when there is so widespread a discontent with 'civilisation.' I do not see any reason for changing the essay, though, no doubt, much might be added to supplement it. What has, however, struck me is that you leave out of account the reason for the greater health, vigor and high spirit of savages (when such conditions exist), and that is the more stringent natural selection among savages owing to the greater hardness of their life. You doubtless know ch. xvii of Westermarck's Moral Ideas, where he shows how widespread among savages (when they have got past the first crude primitive stage), and in the ancient civilisations, was the practice of infanticide applied to inferior babies and the habit of allowing sick persons to die. That was evidently the secret of the natural superiority of the savage and of the men of the old civilisation, for the Greeks and Romans were very stringent in this matter. The flabbiness of the civilised and the prevalence of doctors and hygienists, which you make fun of, is due to the modern tenderness for human life which is afraid to kill off even the most worthless specimens and so lowers the whole level of 'civilised' humanity, Intoduce a New Hardness in this matter and we should return to the high level of savagery, while the doctors would disappear as if by magic. I don't myself believe we can introduce this hardness; and that is why I attach so much importance to intelligent eugenics, working through birth-control, as the only now possible way of getting towards that high natural level you aim at."-Havelock Ellis (1920).

###

Printed in Great Britain
by Amazon